DRAWINGS AND WATERCOLORS
CÉZANNE

DRAWINGS AND WATERCOLORS
CÉZANNE

by Jiří Siblík

3M Books
St. Paul, Minnesota
1984

CÉZANNE: Drawings and Watercolors
by Jiří Siblík

Designer: Milan Hegar
Editor, English language edition: Susan Perry
Supervising editor, English language edition: Pamela Espeland
Translated from the German by Brigitte Edstrom
Designers, jacket and text for English language edition: Evans-Smith & Skubic, Incorporated

---

Library of Congress Cataloging in Publication Data

Siblík, Jiří.
   Cézanne, drawings and watercolors.

   Translation of: Cézanne, zeichnungen und aquarelle.
   Bibliography: p.
   1. Cézanne, Paul, 1839-1906. 2. Art—Psychology.
I. Cézanne, Paul, 1839-1906. II. Title.
N6853.C45S513   1984   759.4   84-8456
ISBN 0-88159-801-1

Distributed to the trade by the Putnam Publishing Group
Printed in Czechoslovakia

CONTENTS

Notes on the Collotype Process

To achieve the most accurate reproductions of Cézanne's drawings possible, the publishers of this volume have elected to use a special photographic process called *collotype*. This expensive and old-fashioned printing method was invented in 1855 and put into commercial use in 1868. At most, it can produce only a few thousand copies, yet because of its ability to render fine detail it remains in demand for short runs of fine art prints of illustrations and for limited editions of books.

A collotype is made on a sheet of ground glass coated with bichromated gelatin. The plate is first dried in an oven until the gelatin reticulates into a pattern of almost microscopic cracks. A continuous-tone negative is then held up to the plate and light is passed through both the plate and the negative, causing the gelatin to harden in direct proportion to the tones of the negative.

Following this step the plate is washed to remove the bichromate and treated with a glycerine solution that moistens the areas which remained less hard after their exposure to light. A greasy lithographic ink is then rolled over the plate. The ink is repelled by the moist areas but accepted by the tiny reticulation cracks of the dry, hardened areas. Finally, paper is pressed against the plate and the image is transferred.

The collotype process is unsuitable for long print runs due to the fact that the delicate gelatin surface begins to slowly deteriorate after approximately one thousand copies are made. Without the gelatin, however, it would not be possible to reproduce with such accuracy the detailing and shading of the original work of art. Thus, while the process does not lend itself to mass production, it does result in superb prints that capture the beauty and intensity of Cézanne's drawings.

For this volume, the collotype process was used to reproduce each of the 66 black-and-white plates. The 16 color plates were reproduced by the more usual method of offset printing.

—S.P.

INTRODUCTION

What matters is not what the artist does, but what he is. What is of interest to us is Cézanne's restless striving— that is what he teaches us.

—Pablo Picasso, 1935

Paul Cézanne did not look the part of a revolutionary. He dressed like a typical member of the French provincial middle class. Nor did he sound like a revolutionary; on the rare occasions when he discussed politics, recalled a friend, he "subscribed wholeheartedly to any reactionary opinion which might establish his 'soundness'." He was always yearning for approval.

Cézanne's actions also belied a revolutionary personality. He was a withdrawn, painfully shy man who could not tolerate the slightest physical touch of another person. "Isolation," he once said, "is all that I'm good for."

Yet Paul Cézanne was a revolutionary: He, more than any other artist, freed modern painters from centuries of constrictive attitudes and rules about art. His paintings, drawings, and watercolors are the spiritual headwaters from which all twentieth-century art movements have flowed.

Paul Cézanne was the great patriarch of modern art.

1

Cézanne's childhood offered scant hint of what was to follow. He was born illegitimately on January 19, 1839 in Aix-en-Provence in southern France. His father, Louise-Auguste Cézanne, was a shrewd, ambitious, self-made man who amassed a considerable fortune, first in the hat-making trade and later in banking. His mother, Anne-Elisabeth-Honorine Aubert, was an illiterate shopgirl. They married when Paul was five and another child, Marie, was three. A second daughter, Rose, was born ten years later.

Paul received an excellent education. After completing grammar school, he entered the Collège Bourbon, Aix's public secondary school. He was a gifted, hardworking student who won many prizes—although only one in drawing.

It was at the Collège Bourbon that Cézanne met Emile Zola, who would become one of France's most popular writers. They formed a deep and lasting friendship which helped shape their lives and, in many ways, their art. "Every holiday, when we were able to escape from our studies," Zola later wistfully recalled, "we ran wild through the countryside. Our great loves at that time were the poets, and for one year Victor Hugo held sway over us like a despot."

But Cézanne was a difficult friend, even in those early days. He was moody, given to sudden exuberances and equally sudden depressions. Zola understood him—at least then. "When he hurts you," Zola wrote to another friend, "you must not blame his heart but rather the evil demon which beclouds his thought."

The idyllic youth of the two friends ended in 1858, just after Cézanne turned 19, when Zola was forced by financial difficulties to move to Paris. With his companion gone, Cézanne became apathetic and listless. "Believe me, I no longer recognize myself," he wrote to Zola in April of 1858. "I am heavy, stupid and slow." Such feelings would haunt him the rest of his life.

Cézanne's dark mood may have contributed to his failing his baccalaureate examination. He tried again, passed with fairly high marks, and entered law school at the University of Aix. His father had insisted that he become a magistrate, believing such an elevated position might open some doors in Aix that had remained closed to the former hat-trader and his family despite their wealth. Even the purchase in 1859 of the Jas de Bouffan, a forty-five acre estate that had once belonged to a French marquis, had failed to raise the Cézannes' social standing.

Paul, however, despised his law studies and secretly began to harbor the hope of becoming an artist. Painting, once a hobby with him, now became a passion. He enrolled in free drawing classes at the Musée Granet in Aix. Then, after passing his first-year law exams, he approached his father about changing his career. Louise-Auguste was appalled. "Child!" he exclaimed. "Think of the future. With genius you die; with money you eat."

The fight over Cézanne's future continued unabated for more than a year. Finally Louise-Auguste relented and, in April of 1861, Cézanne went to Paris.

PROSTRATE MAN

He took a room near Zola's shabby lodgings at 11 rue Soufflot and began attending the Atelier Suisse, a studio where models were available at a low price. There Cézanne prepared for the entrance examination for the Académie des Beaux-Arts, the most influential art school in France.

At 22, Cézanne was tall and broodingly handsome. He was also very inexperienced—at life and at painting. While he had much to learn, he took criticism very badly. Students at the Atelier nicknamed him "l'écorche"—the man without any skin—because of his suspicious, sensitive nature.

Even Zola found his friend increasingly trying to be with, and their relationship started to deteriorate. "He's stiff as a poker," Zola wrote in June of 1861, "inflexible and difficult to handle. Nothing seems to bend him. If, by chance, he does not agree with me about something, he gets carried away, shouts at me that I don't understand and changes the subject. How can one talk to someone like that?"

After a few months in Paris, Cézanne succumbed to depression and self-doubt and returned to Aix. Zola unsuccessfully tried to stop him. "Paul may have the genius of a great painter," he wrote in despair, "but he will never have the genius to become one."

In Aix, Cézanne went to work as a clerk in his father's bank. But he detested the business world, and the artist in him quickly resurfaced. He set up a studio at the Jas de Bouffan and enrolled again in drawing classes. Soon even Louise-Auguste came to realize that it was no good trying to make a businessman out of his son. In November of 1862, Cézanne moved back to Paris with the guarantee of a small allowance from his father. He never again gave up painting.

Almost immediately after arriving in Paris, Cézanne took and failed the entrance examination to the Académie des Beaux-Arts. His work was much too erotic and violent for the staid, conservative school. Nor were any of his paintings accepted into the Académie's Salon, the all-powerful annual exhibition that dictated popular taste in art.

Then, in the spring of 1863, under pressure from artists whose works had been repeatedly turned down by the official Salon, Napoleon III authorized the opening of the Salon des Refusés. Artists whose paintings had been rejected by the Académie's jury were asked to exhibit; Cézanne was among them.

The Salon des Refusés was a critical flop, and Cézanne's paintings were largely ignored. Yet through the exhibition Cézanne came to know some of the leading anti-Establishment painters of his generation: Edouard Manet (1832-1883), Claude Monet (1840-1926), Armand Guillaumin (1841-1927), Frédéric Bazille (1841-1871), Pierre-Auguste Renoir (1841-1919), Alfred Sisley (1839-1899), and Edgar Degas (1834-1917).

These rebellious painters were known as "the Batignolles" because they met informally at the Café Guerbois in the Batignolles area of Paris. Manet, the son of a well-to-do bourgeois father, was their undisputed leader. Zola often joined the group at the Café; he was now working for a newspaper and frequently championed the Batignolles in the press.

Cézanne, on the other hand, seemed to go out of his way to appear vulgar and defiant among his colleagues. When an opinion he did not like was expressed at the Café Guerbois, he would either viciously attack it or abruptly and icily leave. He loathed pretentious conversations—and pretentious artists. Manet in particular annoyed him with his elegant demeanor and dress. Once, upon entering the Café, Cézanne shook hands with everyone except Manet. "I do not shake your hand, Monsieur Manet," he said, pulling in peasant fashion at his trousers and accentuating his nasal Provençal accent. "I have not washed for a week."

In 1870, Napoleon III declared war on Prussia and the Batignolles disbanded. To avoid the draft, Cézanne went into hiding in L'Estaque, a village just outside Marseilles. He took with him his 20-year-old mistress, Marie-Hortense Fiquet.

She earned her living in Paris by sewing bindings on books and may have also modeled for Cézanne. She was a dark, strong-jawed woman, apparently gregarious but uninterested in art. Cézanne's friends made fun of her and called her "La Boule"—the Ball—perhaps because they felt she fettered the artist and his work. Cézanne himself often spoke derisively of Hortense, but he seemed to have had a genuine, if curious, affection for her.

After the war with Prussia came to its swift and disastrous end, Cézanne returned to Paris. A few months later his son, Paul, was born. The birth complicated Cézanne's personal life. Paris was getting on his nerves; he longed to retreat to the country, as he did almost every summer. If he went south, however, his father would surely find out about his family and cut off his allowance. It had been relatively easy to conceal a mistress on his annual sojourns to Aix; a mother and child were another matter, however.

The problem was solved when Camille Pissarro invited Cézanne, Hortense, and the baby to his home at Pontoise in the Oise valley. The visit had a profound effect on Cézanne. Perceptive and tactful, Pissarro persuaded the younger artist to tone down his violent style, to use lighter, brighter colors, and to create form with color as well as line. "He was a father to me," Cézanne later recalled, "a man you could ask about anything, like God."

Pissarro and Cézanne spent hours painting in the countryside around Pontoise and the nearby village of Auvers, to which Cézanne moved in 1873. Other artists from the Batignolles group—Renoir, Degas, Manet, and Monet—had also left their Paris studios to pursue the then-radical idea of painting out-of-doors. They wanted to capture nature as it really appeared to them in its fleeting, ever-changing forms. "One does not paint a landscape, a seascape, a figure," said Manet. "One paints an impression of an hour of the day."

In 1874, the Impressionists, as they were soon to be termed, held their first group exhibition in Paris. Three of Cézanne's paintings were shown, despite the objections of other contributors who feared that his work was too unconventional even for such an avant-garde exhibition.

The show received bad reviews. Cézanne's paintings in particular were viciously attacked. One critic called him "a sort of madman who paints in delirium tremens." Cézanne contributed paintings and watercolors to two more group shows of the Impressionists, and each time his work was ridiculed.

In the late 1870s, angered by the public's rejection, Cézanne went into a self-imposed exile that lasted for almost 20 years. Most of those were spent in his beloved Provence. His friends were few; of the Batignolles group, only Pissarro, Renoir, and Monet visited him regularly. Many people actually thought he had died.

While in seclusion, Cézanne matured as a painter. He quickly outgrew Impressionism, which he considered too superficial. He wanted to delve more deeply beneath the surface of a scene to find its underlying structure. He tried, as he pointed out in one of his most celebrated comments, to "see in nature the cylinder, the sphere, the cone." He attempted to reduce scenes to their most simple geometric forms.

At the same time, his personal life became more complicated. Louise-Auguste learned about Hortense and the child and cut his son's allowance in half. Cézanne was forced to borrow money from Zola. "My good family, which is very worthy, to be sure," he wrote with dry understatement, "is perhaps a bit tight-fisted to an unfortunate painter who has never been able to do anything."

Cézanne finally married Hortense in 1886 for reasons that remain unclear. The marriage seems to have been connected to a mysterious love affair that Cézanne may have had with a maid at the Jas de Bouffan in the summer of 1885. Although little is known about the affair, it appears that Cézanne's father discovered it too, and abruptly dismissed the maid, much to Cézanne's dismay. The episode propelled the artist into a deep and sustained depression. Between May and August of 1885, he did not paint at all; this was the only nonproductive period of his life. The affair may also have prompted Cézanne's family to insist on a marriage with Hortense.

Six months after the wedding, Cézanne's father died. At the age of 47, Cézanne found himself financially independent at last. Yet this did not bring him either happiness or peace. That same year—1886—saw the publication of Zola's novel *L'Oeuvre (The Masterpiece)*, an event that marked the end of Cézanne's long friendship with him. The protagonist, Claude Lantier, was "a great painter who failed," "an incomplete genius." Although the book was labeled a work of fiction, few people were fooled: Lantier was none other than Paul Cézanne.

The artist was hurt and offended. After receiving a copy of the book from Zola, he wrote his friend a final, formal note: "My Dear Emile, I have just received *L'Oeuvre*, which you were kind enough to send me. I thank the author of *Les Rougon-Macquart* for this token of remembrance, and I beg him to allow me to shake his hand to commemorate past years. Yours ever, in memory of the old days. Paul Cézanne."

Now it was Zola's turn to be hurt. He had in his possession a number of Cézanne's paintings, and he ordered them to be taken down from the walls of his house and put in the attic. The two men never spoke or wrote to each other again.

Cézanne alienated other old friends as well, including Pissarro, Monet, and Renior. He became more and more sullen and suspicious, especially around other artists. "They think I've got a secret formula, and they want to steal it from me," he charged. "But I've got rid of them all, and not one of them, not one, will get hold of me!" Some of Cézanne's increased irritability was probably a result of the diabetes that struck him in his later years.

Cézanne was happiest at the Jas de Bouffan, where he secluded himself for long periods with his mother and his sister Marie. Hortense preferred Paris; she

PAGE FROM A SKETCHBOOK

and Cézanne seldom spent time together anymore. She continued to pose for her husband when they did and was one of the few people who could meet his strict demands for immobility. In all, Cézanne did 27 paintings of her.

Gradually, almost in spite of himself, Cézanne began to become famous. In 1895, the art dealer Ambroise Vollard organized a Paris exhibition of his works. It included 150 canvases painted from 1868 to 1894. The reviews were mixed. "The dilettantes are astounded and cannot understand a thing," wrote the ever-faithful Pissarro to his son, "but it is great painting nevertheless. It has a staggering delicacy, diversity and classicism...My enthusiasm is nothing compared with Renoir's. Even Degas has fallen under the spell of this sensitive savage. Monet, everyone. We may be mistaken, but I doubt it."

Other exhibitions followed, and a few prescient collectors began buying his works in large quantities. Vollard went to Cézanne's studio in 1897 and prudently purchased every painting, drawing, and watercolor he found there.

For Cézanne, however, fame arrived too late. It had eluded him for years; now it no longer interested him.

In 1897, Cézanne's mother died. Two years later, against his wishes, his sister sold the Jas de Bouffan. Cézanne moved into an apartment in Aix and bought an acre of land on the outskirts of the town, where he built a studio. He painted there in the mornings; in the afternoons, he wandered the countryside with his easel, painting "on the motif."

Old age, the passage of time, death—these themes seemed to obsess him during the last years of his life. "How many memories have been engulfed in the abyss of the years!" he wrote to his son Paul. Zola, who had shared many of those memories, died on September 28, 1902. "Go away, go away!" Cézanne is said to have tearfully shouted at the gardener who brought him the news. He then locked himself in his studio for the remainder of the day.

His own death came four years later. "I have sworn to die painting, rather than waste away in the debasing paralysis which threatens old men," he wrote to a friend in September of 1906. Within a month, he collapsed while returning home in a sudden rainstorm from an outdoor painting session. He was taken in a coma to his apartment.

On the following day, he insisted on going to his studio to work on a portrait, but became ill and had to return home. Irascible to the end, he wrote an angry letter—his last—to his color merchant in Paris: "It is now eight days since I asked you to send me ten burnt lakes No. 7, and I have had no reply. What is the matter? A reply, please, and a quick one...."

Cézanne died five days later, on October 22, 1906, of pneumonia complicated by diabetes. He was 67 years old. In 1907, a retrospective of his works was held in Paris to considerable critical acclaim.

THE DRAWINGS AND WATERCOLORS OF CÉZANNE

Drawing and color are by no means two different things. As you paint, you draw.
—Paul Cézanne

Few artists experienced as much disappointment in their lives as Paul Cézanne; few were as mocked as he. It was only after his death in 1906 that Cézanne's work was widely recognized as that of a great master.

Many of his contemporaries were unsure of his talent. These included the group of painters who would soon be known as the Impressionists. Cézanne was influenced by them when he first moved to Paris in 1861 at the urging of his boyhood friend, Emile Zola. In fact, it was the Impressionist painter Camille Pissarro who introduced Cézanne to *plein-air* painting, or painting out-of-doors—a revolutionary idea in mid-nineteenth century France. But Cézanne quickly developed his own distinctive style, which went far beyond Impressionism and made him the true pioneer of modern painting.

The public was critical of his paintings and even less receptive to his drawings and watercolors. Cézanne's drawings were viewed as transitional pieces rather than complete works, and consequently dismissed as unimportant. Yet Cézanne drew throughout his life and considered drawing essential to his development as an artist.

Much of his personality is revealed in the lines of his drawings. Plagued by indecision and self-doubt, mistrustful of others and painfully shy, he found it difficult to express himself with clarity and confidence. These characteristics are evident in his frequently vague outlines, to which he sometimes added color in an attempt at better definition. Some critics have said that Cézanne destroyed the outlines of the objects he painted to give his works more softness and freedom. The painter Fernand Léger (1881-1955) came closer to the truth when he observed that Cézanne did not actually "destroy" outlines; rather, he depicted them as they are perceived in nature

9

by the human eye—as differentiations of color, not as lines.

The Impressionists were not alone in judging Cézanne's approach to painting hard to comprehend. Even today, his work is often misunderstood. As the artist himself said, "I was born too early!" Indeed, he was born too soon to reap the kind of recognition he deserved—but he arrived on the scene just in time to introduce the world to a new era of painting. His work paved the way for modern art. As the art critic Lionello Venturi noted, no artist had such close ties with his successors as did Paul Cézanne.

Cézanne never founded an art "school" in either the literal or figurative sense of the term, nor has one come into being since his death. But his "students" may be found in all modern art movements—from Fauvism, Cubism and Orphism to German Expressionism and Surrealism. Indeed, it is difficult to find a major modern artist or movement that has not been influenced by Cézanne. He was, as the great Fauvist Henri Matisse (1869-1954) said, "the father of us all."

Some of the artists who have followed Cézanne have considered his work the climax of classicism, seeing in his paintings the renewal of forgotten laws. Others have viewed Cézanne as a revolutionary who abolished those laws. But all, despite these differing perspectives, have called Paul Cézanne their spiritual father, tracing their artistic intuitions back to him.

According to artist Maurice Denis (1870-1943), a friend of Cézanne's and the painter of the famous group portrait, *Homage to Cézanne* (1900), the artist was both "complex and versatile." Because he was so complex, artists who came after him have been able to find in his work almost everything they have looked for—including a number of things that are not there. Yet even misinterpretations of Cézanne's work have led to new artistic directions and discoveries.

Part of the confusion concerning the interpretation of Cézanne's work had its origins in comments the artist himself made. His desire for approval sometimes led him to say what a listener wanted to hear, regardless of whether it was true. Furthermore, he was often not able to clearly express his artistic intentions. As Denis once remarked, "Cézanne was a thinker, but he did not always think the same thing every day."

An art scholar said about Cézanne, "Er weiss nichts, sein Genius erraet alles" ("He does not know anything; his genius is guessing everything"). His genius, at least, cannot be questioned. Like Ludwig van Beethoven had done for composers half a century earlier, Cézanne cut a new path for artists. Each man worked in solitude, living almost exclusively for his art. Each paid a huge emotional price on the way to finishing a masterpiece. Each had a strong personal belief in his artistic mission.

In Cézanne's case, that belief was undermined throughout his life by insecurities. As a result, every painting posed a new problem—a problem that could be solved only with great difficulty, persistence, and pain.

10

Cézanne's drawings are the most impressive evidence of his fight to overcome artistic problems. But even when his paintings were beginning to gain some recognition—which happened toward the end of his life—his drawings remained unknown and underestimated. It was claimed that Cézanne did not know how to draw. This claim, however, was more reflective of the attitude toward drawing that existed at the time than of Cézanne's abilities.

At the beginning of the twentieth century, sketches, studies, and rough drafts were considered important to the painter and no one else. Such works were to be concealed from the public, since they revealed the artist's "weaknesses" as he searched for a final expression. "One can compare [drawings] with the first words of an author," wrote the art critic Camille Mauclair in 1907. "They remain outside his works....Neither the public nor the critics are entitled to them; they belong exclusively to the biographer and the artist's friends."

Even if early twentieth-century critics had felt differently about drawings, they still would not have understood the drawings of Cézanne. His works were not based on the traditional linear concept, in which forms have sharp outlines and the viewer's eye is directed along a defined course. In Cézanne's drawings, line performs a new, nonlinear function.

Lines between objects do not exist in nature, he pointed out; they are invented by artists to express the three-dimensional correlations between color and light. He argued that the infinite diversity of these correlations cannot be expressed by a single, continuous, and firmly contoured line. So he deemphasized his outlines, allowing the viewer's eye to wander more freely over his forms. And that is why it was said that he could not draw. Some of his contemporaries who considered his paintings "the worst joke of the century" believed his drawings not worth mentioning at all.

Cézanne did not draw like any artist before him because he did not want to. He chose instead to develop his own unique style. He saw drawing as a means of studying "un rapport de contraste ou simplement le rapport de deux tons, le blanc et le noir" ("the relationship between contrasts or simply between two tones, black and white"). He wanted to be aware of those two extremes at all times, even when painting with oils. When he was a young man painting at the Atelier Suisse in Paris, he always placed a black hat and a white handkerchief next to his model as reminders.

He also formulated a new approach to the problem of perspective in painting. As the art scholar Fritz Novotny has written, Cézanne's style marked "the end of the scientific perspective." Novotny was referring to the mathematically-based system of linear perspective first developed by artists in the fifteenth century. This system used converging and diverging lines to create an illusion of three-dimensional depth on a two-dimensional canvas. By drawing objects progressively smaller and closer together toward the horizon, or "rear" of the painting, objects were made to appear as though they were receding in space.

Cézanne rejected this formulaic approach. It restricted him too much. He wanted each object he depicted to have the size he felt it deserved as part of the general motif of his painting. Yet he did not believe that a painting should appear entirely flat; in fact, he once accused Paul Gauguin (1848-1903) of neglecting depth in his works. Cézanne challenged all painters to create a sense of depth while at the same time remaining faithful to the two-dimensional surface of the canvas.

He did not use space to create an optical illusion; he did not want to distract the viewer from this two-dimensional reality. That is why "mistakes" appear in his paintings—why table edges and pottery rims seem misdrawn and houses appear slanted. To Cézanne, even the air was an object, a material substance connecting people and things.

He frequently worked out problems of perspective in his drawings. He also drew as a way of searching for elements with which to build his paintings, much as a poet searches for words with which to create a poem. Cézanne's drawings are studies of trees and rocks, of shapes and moods, of men and women, of the multi-colored relationship between foreground and background. They are incomplete yet whole in that each carries the full message the artist wished to express. Only rarely did Cézanne "finish" a drawing in the traditional sense, scorning what he termed "the perfection of the feeble-minded."

Just as a handwriting analyst can identify personality traits through signatures or writing specimens, one who knows something of Cézanne's life can read his temperament in his drawings. Bent lines reveal his self-doubt and inconsistency. Double lines reveal his fear of making decisions. When he drew with the tip of his pencil, the motion was never hard and sharp but soft and indulgent, evidencing his lack of self-assurance. It is because Cézanne's drawings tell us so much about the man as well as the artist that we devote so much attention to them.

In 1936, Venturi listed Cézanne's extant works as consisting of 800 oil paintings, 350 watercolors, and 350 drawings. Today approximately 1000 drawings are accounted for. The Kupferstichkabinett der Oeffentlichen Kunstsammlung (Copper Engravings Cabinet) of the Kunstmuseum in Basel, Switzerland owns 211 of these (a total of 142 pages, of which 70 have drawings on both sides). The rest are scattered around the world, making it difficult to study them.

Even if all of Cézanne's known drawings could be collected, no museum has enough room to keep them on constant display. And even if one did, the brittle paper they are drawn on would not long survive intense illumination. Books such as this offer the easiest way to familiarize oneself with this aspect of the master's work.

SELF-PORTRAIT

We would have far more drawings to study and enjoy had Cézanne not destroyed many of them (along with many of his unfinished paintings) near the end of his life. He had come to distrust the small but growing number of people who suddenly wanted to buy his works. One such foresighted man was the art dealer Ambroise

Vollard. Vollard organized Cézanne's first one-man show in 1895 at the suggestion of Camille Pissarro. The show was a success and marked the beginning of Cézanne's fame as a painter. Two years later, Vollard went to Cézanne's studio and bought everything he could talk Cézanne into selling him , including damaged paintings and small sketches.

Had Cézanne been younger, he might have gained some self-confidence as a result of this enthusiasm for his work. But he had met with so many failures and disappointments in the past that he feared Vollard's motives. "He's up to something, something criminal," Cézanne remarked about the art dealer. Not wanting Vollard to get hold of those works he felt were "unrealized," he burned them. Besides, what did the praise of an art dealer matter when the director of the museum in Aix-en-Provence—Cézanne's home town—had sworn that no work of Cézanne's would hang on the museum's walls while he, the director, was still alive? Like many others, the director considered Cézanne too revolutionary. Cézanne wore this adjective unwillingly; he longed for official recognition.

Cézanne was careless with his drawings. Never totally satisfied with them, he left them strewn about the floor or misplaced them. Vollard recalled how Renoir returned from a visit to the artist "with a beautiful watercolor which [Cézanne] forgot between rocks, after he slaved over it at least twenty times." Cézanne's indifference to his drawings was due to the fact that he focused his vision on the final goal—the finished painting. His drawings and incomplete paintings were embarrassing testimony to his frequent artistic defeats. He did not want to be reminded of these disappointments, so he neglected many of his efforts, discarding drawings and canvases outdoors at the sites where he had struggled so intensely with them. Inside his apartment, disorder reigned. As Henri Perruchot noted in his book about Cézanne, there were only a few pieces of furniture—"a sink, a couch, an old box and a stove." But there were "brushes all over, empty color tubes and mountains of drawings."

Cézanne drew all his life. When he was not painting, he was capturing everything in sight in drawings. This was especially true during the first stage of his artistic career (1858-1871), when his work was still Impressionless and his concept of line had not yet achieved its relation to color. Unfortunately, few of his early drawings have survived. His Impressionistic period (1872-1877) saw his only genuine lapse from the habit of drawing. This was unremarkable, given that none of the other Impressionists drew very much; for example, Claude Monet and Alfred Sisley never drew, and Renoir sketched for only a short time. A pencil was not suited to capturing the fleeting game of light.

The majority of Cézanne's remaining drawings are from 1880-1895, when the man matured as an artist. These were most often sketched with a lead pencil and enhanced with watercolor. His later drawings form a bridge between his earlier efforts and the watercolors of his final years.

He may have considered the drawings themselves as not worth saving, but Cézanne nevertheless valued the process of drawing and what he learned from it. To him, a drawing was a preliminary yet independent step toward a painting. Unlike most painters, however, Cézanne never drew in order to later reproduce the drawing in color (oils). His drawings were color problems whose solutions lay in the details he added to them. He viewed drawing as a simple exercise, yet he approached it with as much energy and commitment as he approached the act of painting and worked just as hard at it. Drawing also afforded him variety, a different means of expression. Often he drew in his "free moments"—times when he could not paint; for example, in the evenings, while sitting at his table.

Frequently, he dismissed his drawings as failures. When his mother lay dying, he tried to draw her but eventually threw away his pencil and asked another artist, Joseph Villevieille (1821-1916), to make the sketch for him.

Cézanne's artistic style was so misunderstood that it was once suggested that he suffered from a vision defect. Only such a defect, said his critics, could explain his distorted way of seeing, his "misdrawings."

Of course it was not his eyesight but his inner vision that resulted in his revolutionary approach to drawing. He had a wholly original concept of the meaning of line. For centuries, a continuous line had been considered more important than color. A neatly executed drawing was believed essential to a painting. The Impressionists, seeking to free color from its subordinate role, rejected linear drawing altogether, claiming that it "strangulates the shapes as with wire."

Cézanne also emphasized color, but without rejecting drawing. It still served a basic function in his art, although after his Impressionistic period it took on new meaning. While his contemporaries dissolved shapes in favor of color, Cézanne directed his efforts toward forming shapes by using color rather than line as his primary means of modeling. He wanted to turn Impressionism into a classical art, to make of it "something solid and durable, like the art of the Museums."

Color did not take the place of line in Cézanne's work; it simply pushed line into the background. Or, more precisely, it merged with line to create a unified sense of shape. "Drawing and color," he insisted, "are by no means two different things. As you paint, you draw. The more harmoniously colors are combined, the more clearly outlines stand out. When color is at its richest, form is at its fullest."

He always claimed to enjoy the line. At the same time, he accused Raphael (1483-1520), Hans Holbein the Younger (1497-1543), François Clouet (1520-1572), and Jean Auguste Dominique Ingres (1780-1867) of knowing nothing *but* the line. For Cézanne, drawing was never an ultimate goal, never an end in itself. It was only the first step in the use of color. He was always thinking of color, even when drawing with the pencil.

An artist, Cézanne once observed, "experiences joy when he is able to communicate to his fellow human beings his enthusiasm for the masterly works of nature, the secret of which he is trying to find." He felt this joy of communication in his drawings as well as his paintings, if on a somewhat less glorious scale. Drawing was intended to capture "les petites sensations"—the small experiences.

Cézanne never intended his drawings for public viewing; they were his own private, indispensable tools. Through them he studied his models and captured and organized his experiences, albeit the small ones, for future reference. Only rarely did he use a sketchbook; most of his drawings were done on loose pages, and he often used both sides. When the public did see Cézanne's drawings, it reacted as negatively as it had to his paintings. But despite repeated charges that he couldn't draw, Cézanne persisted in pursuing his artistic vision.

Actually, his early works proved that he could not only draw but draw "right." His deviations from classical linear perspective and anatomical laws were deliberate, not accidental. "The artist does not work like a bird sings," he explained. "He composes." In other words, there was reasoned order, not randomness, behind his art. His drawings differed from those of traditional painters, but it was not through lack of discipline or incompetency.

For many artists, the first attempt at capturing an experience of the senses usually results in a drawing—a study in which impressions are analyzed and ordered. Cézanne's drawings helped him to analyze and order his "color experiences." Often the color is only hinted at by the shadings of a black pencil. These shadings, which take the form of a mass of lines, surround the shaky outlines of objects. Light and dark tones are indicated through the pressure of the pencil.

Novotny wrote, "The line which surrounds the objects in continuously changing grades of intensity arrives sometimes at a rich graphic expression; at other times, it weakens to a vague approximation at the cautious touching of two color areas, or it disappears completely in certain areas." Cézanne's line does not separate objects; rather, it helps connect them.

Shadows play a decisive role in both his paintings and drawings. His compositions generally consist of an arrangement of colored shadows on which everything depends. In observing shapes, Cézanne found that the side in the light appeared bigger and more expansive while the side in the dark appeared smaller and more limited. He made each of his objects protrude out of shadow.

Cézanne's line varied from one drawing to the next. It was either hard and rigid or vague and interrupted, disappearing and reappearing as if in a fog. Usually it was the latter. This vagueness stemmed from the artist's new concept of how two objects are bordered in space—the concept that color differences, not artificially inserted lines, define the perimeters of objects. Traditionally, such color differences were divided from each other, communicating the prevailing feelings of conviction, steadiness, and tranquility. By the end of the nineteenth century, however, world events had replaced these feelings with doubt, dissatisfaction, and insecurity. For an artist like Cézanne, who was deeply attached to his times, these changes had great significance.

Some art scholars have seen similarities between Cézanne's drawing style and that of the restless Baroque painters of the seventeenth century, most notably Pierre Puget (1620-1694) and Peter Paul Rubens (1577-1640). Baroque artists blended light, color, and movement in an attempt to make a direct and overpowering emotional appeal to the viewer. In painting, they expressed their restlessness via abundant ornaments; in music, through the wanderings of the sixteenth note.

But a style cannot be precisely repeated or transferred from one era to another. We must therefore resist the temptation to align Cézanne with a period long gone. Although many of his drawings had their origins in his admiration for Baroque painters, this by no means proves that he preferred the decorative Baroque style. Any Baroque-like elements in his paintings cannot be said to reflect the empty splendor of a past century; instead, they mirror the restless, doubting spirit of the artist's own milieu.

As noted earlier, Cézanne used drawing as a preliminary step toward painting. But not all of his drawings are directly related to specific paintings and most, in fact, were never transferred to canvas. Each one, however, is at least indirectly connected to his paintings insofar as it contains the solution to one or more artistic problems.

To simplify matters, we may divide his drawings into two categories: those that are directly related to his paintings, and those that are not. The first category consists of sketches from nature which capture the "correlation of things," to use art scholar Gertrude Berthold's phrase. The second consists of sketches from other pieces of finished art. Drawings in the latter category may be considered independent works. Through them, Cézanne studied individual figures, body positions, movements, and gestures.

The difference between these two categories is significant. The drawings from nature are concerned with entire compositions, complete thoughts Cézanne wanted to visualize. They explore the main points needed for the plasticity—or three-dimensional effect—of a painting.

In contrast, the drawings from existing works of art contain only isolated elements. Cézanne did most of these in the Louvre in Paris, which he visited regularly when he was unable to venture out into nature. He felt comfortable in the museum.

The paintings and plaster-of-Paris castings were easier to work with than restless models. Many of Cézanne's museum drawings remind us of those made by all art students, but they had great meaning for him. Through them, he stabilized his views and attitudes.

He enjoyed sketching from sculptured works, especially antique marble statues. Because of their relative lack of color, such statues are well suited to the pencil. They presented Cézanne with a unique opportunity to study the play of light and shadow. He also liked sculpture because he could view the object from various angles and observe the changes in light.

Cézanne never randomly chose a statue to sketch; he always had a certain problem in mind he wanted to solve. In addition to antique statues, he frequently turned to the works of Michelangelo (1475-1564), Jean-Antoine Houdon (1741-1828), and Germain Pilon (c. 1531-1580).

Cézanne was not interested in reproducing on paper an entire sculpture he found in the Louvre, nor did he care to make exact copies of the paintings he sketched there. Rather, he went to the Louvre to study details, in particular details of the human body. He preferred the Louvre to his studio for obvious reasons. The museum was quiet; it contained a large selection of details to study; and the models were eternally patient and motionless. Cézanne could work undisturbed for hours. Best of all, he did not have to feel shy before the silent, unquestioning statues.

At the beginning of his career, Cézanne alternated between sketching from nature and sketching in the Louvre. Often his mood for the day was determined by how well his morning's work had gone at the Louvre. Vollard remarked that Cézanne had to be satisfied with the drawings he made there or he could not paint at all.

Vollard was probably right. The significance of the role the museum played in Cézanne's life was made clear in a 1905 letter to the painter Emile Bernard (1868-1941). "The Louvre," Cézanne wrote, "is a book in which we learn how to read."

Cézanne's love of drawing sprang from a number of childhood sources. At around the age of five, he started to draw in play. He spent hours copying pictures from *Magasin Pittoresque*, a periodical his family subscribed to. But neither Paul nor his parents credited this early interest with much importance.

While attending a grammar school in Saint-Joseph, Cézanne took drawing lessons with a Spanish monk as a mandatory part of the curriculum. When he was 13 he entered the Collège Bourbon, where painting and drawing were voluntary subjects, and chose to study them there. He excelled in painting but failed in drawing. In fact, drawing was the only subject he did not do well in; he was, for example, an excellent Latin student. His friend, Emile Zola, won a prize one year in drawing; Cézanne won none.

PAGE FROM A SKETCHBOOK

Both Cézanne and Zola were at that time determined to become poets, not painters. They were taken with the romantic poems of Alfred de Musset (1810-1857) and Victory Hugo (1802-1885) and could often be found tramping across the countryside surrounding Aix-en-Provence, shouting verse at each other.

They did not neglect their drawing, however. In the fall of 1858, when Cézanne was 19, he enrolled in Aix's Drawing School, which was run by the director of the city's Musée Granet. Joseph Gibert (1808-1884), the director, was the school's art instructor and an academic portrait painter as well. Although Cézanne's father considered painting a useless occupation, he did see its merits in the schooling of a gentleman and made no objection when Paul voiced his intent to study. Besides, he would rather Paul draw in the evenings than lounge about idly in local cafés—and, as an added bonus, the school was free. Louise-Auguste Cézanne may also have taken some degree of pleasure in the little watercolors that Paul's sister Marie turned out.

At the Drawing School, Cézanne met others who were preparing to make a career of art: Auguste Truphémus, the brother of the sculptor François Truphémus; Numa Costa, son of a poor shoemaker; Joseph Villevieille, who was ten years Paul's senior; and the talented Joseph Huot. It was fortunate that he had such stimulating classmates, for the museum itself had little to offer that could expand the young painter's artistic ideas and impulses. Only one painting, *The Card Players*, which is generally attributed to Luis Le Nain (c. 1593-1648), caught Cézanne's attention and remained in his memory for the rest of his life.

The youth made good progress under Gibert. At the Collège Bourbon, he finally won a second prize in drawing. He had to struggle to pass the baccalaureate examination, however. He failed the first time but passed the follow-up exams in time to enter the University of Aix school of law in the fall of 1858. His father had insisted that he go.

During the two years he spent at law school, Cézanne continued with his drawing, frequently working with live models. Gradually the thought of becoming an artist took shape in his mind. He wrote to Zola, who had moved to Paris with his mother, and asked him for information about entering the powerful and influential Académie des Beaux-Arts. Then he paused, reluctant to take any direct action that might displease his father. He knew that Louise-Auguste wanted an honorable lawyer, not a second-rate painter, for a son.

Still, Cézanne could not suppress his need to paint. He decided to test his abilities by painting a folding screen for his father's study at the Jas de Bouffan, his family's country estate near Aix. His father had bought the estate in 1859. A drive lined with chestnut trees led to the mansion, which was surrounded by a 37-acre park. Paul never left the house without his sketchbook or a stretched canvas; from his drawings and paintings, it is apparent that the estate contained a park overgrown with weeds, a pond, and surrounding meadows and vineyards.

Cézanne went on to paint four panels inside the mansion. Completed in 1860, and called "The Four Seasons," they are characteristic of his work because they reflect his personality. Meanwhile Zola waited impatiently in Paris, wanting his friend's company to make the city more bearable for him. He did not have long to wait. Cézanne felt artistically cramped at Aix; he wanted—and needed— to go to Paris. There he hoped to get the expert instruction that would point his talent in the right direction. His father finally yielded to his wishes, but only because he believed that the disappointments and defeats Paul would doubtless experience in Paris would bring him to his senses and back to a career in law and business.

Cézanne arrived in Paris in 1861, hoping to be accepted into the Académie des Beaux-Arts. To prepare for the entrance examination, he studied earnestly at the Atelier Suisse. It was a studio, not a school, and had no professors or exams, but it provided live models.

One of the students at the Atelier was a hunchbacked dwarfish man named Achille Emperaire. Cézanne was intrigued by him and the two became friends. Other students included Antoine Guillemet (1841-1918) and Camille Pissarro, the latter of whom recognized Cézanne's unique talent and encouraged him. Cézanne desperately needed the older man's kind words, for he was often deeply depressed.

It was around this time that his friendship with Zola began to suffer.

Cézanne was very unhappy with his painting and, as a result, increasingly obstinate and difficult to be around. "If he advances an inconsistent opinion and you dispute it," Zola wrote to Baptistin Baille, a mutual friend from Aix, "he flies into a rage...screams that you know nothing about the subject and jumps to something else."

Cézanne finally succumbed to his feelings of worthlessness and returned to Aix, much to the satisfaction of his father. Louise-Auguste believed that his son had once and for all given up the rebellious notion of becoming a painter. Paul began working in his father's bank, patiently studying papers and figures and calculations. He seemed vanquished.

His desire to paint surfaced again, however, and he was soon enrolled in drawing classes and meeting with his artist friends. He even set up a private studio in the Jas de Bouffan.

Filled with renewed strength and hope, he made another journey to Paris. For the rest of his life, he would continue in this manner, torn between two towns. In Paris, he would be unhappy and homesick for Aix; in Aix, he would crave the excitement and stimulation of Paris.

During his second stay in Paris, Cézanne returned to the Atelier Suisse. He worked a regular schedule, from 8 a.m. to 1 p.m. and then from 7 p.m. to 10 p.m. Pissarro assumed his former role as advisor and mentor. When Cézanne failed the entrance exam to the Académie des Beaux Arts, Pissarro consoled him and helped him to recognize the uselessness of the "sterile" education taught at the Académie. Cézanne, after all, was striving for an energetic, living art, not a cliché. In the end, the Louvre was Cézanne's school.

Not receiving a classical education proved to have both advantages and disadvantages. It enabled Cézanne to preserve his spontaneity; it also made his work harder because he never learned technical skills or tricks. Throughout his career, he would have to struggle to express his concepts. But struggle he did; he was never lazy.

The drawings from these early years represent a very important part of Cézanne's work. Unfortunately, as noted earlier, most were destroyed and it is now impossible to adequately judge their quality. Already, however, Cézanne seemed to have rejected the smooth and elegant lines of painters like Ingres. He preferred brash color-masters like Eugene Delacroix (1798-1863), whom he considered the symbol of artistic courage and freedom. He related to Rubens, the "great decorative master," and to Poussin (1594-1665).

In this stage of his career, Cézanne used long, solid lines to render the shapes of things. After 1876, his lines became shorter, disconnected—hints of their former selves.

During the second period of his artistic development (1872-1877), Cézanne garnered moral support from his Impressionistic friends. He also learned a great deal from them, especially from Pissarro, who taught him to observe nature with patience, devotion, and acute attentiveness.

While under the sway of Impressionism, Cézanne drew little. Mostly he painted and learned how to control his temperament on canvas.

Cézanne succumbed to the influence of Impressionism for only a short time. Although he considered nature the primary prerequisite to a work of art, he wanted to record lasting values, not fleeting impressions. Rather than capturing a brief, single moment, he wanted to recreate a synthesis of several moments. He worked on his paintings much longer than his Impressionistic colleagues. Often he had to paint artificial flowers because real ones would wilt before he was done.

Cézanne continued to spend much of his time in the Louvre, where he thought about his art and compared his work to that of the past. He discovered the sixteenth-century artists who comprised what is now referred to as the Venetian school of painting. These artists had discarded the traditional attitude that color was merely a decorative element and had used it as a structural tool, building layer upon layer of rich, warm, almost golden tones. Next to nature, the Venetians became Cézanne's most important source of inspiration.

The majority of Cézanne's extant drawings date from his later years, when he matured as an artist. The scholar Lionello Venturi has divided these years into two periods: constructive (1878-1887) and synthetic (1888-1906). During the former, according to Venturi, Cézanne worked on formal problems, primarily composition; during the latter, he synthesized formal and semantic problems and approached them simultaneously. Throughout both periods, Cézanne's paintings and drawings followed a mutual path, accompanying and complementing each other. Edgar Degas once said that "the drawing is not a shape, but a way to see the shape;" a description that fits Cézanne's later drawings.

Cézanne never considered a shape as something firm having a precise border. He saw each object as if it were a gem with many facets, none dominant. He liked to give his objects two or more edges. In doing so, he was being imprecise, not incomplete.

His self-doubt played a significant role in his attitude toward shaping objects. If his life could not follow a straight, secure line, how could his objects? If he could not make decisions in a clear, energetic, unconditional manner, how could he express the outlines of drawn objects with single, firm, determined lines? Instead, he used bundles of lines, often complaining about "outlines which run away."

To categorize Cézanne's drawings chronologically is an impossible task. The artist never dated his oil paintings, much less his drawings. The difficulty of assigning dates to the drawings is further exacerbated by the fact that Cézanne often used both sides of his drawing paper—and at different times. Nor can his drawings be sorted according to the presumed dates of his oil paintings, for they seldom appear to relate directly to individual paintings. Drawings that are clearly related to paintings were usually sketched before the paintings were completed—but some came after. The latter served as transitions to new solutions for the same problems.

Cézanne drew primarily with a pencil. It was soft and manageable, although not as soft as charcoal, which smudged easily. Undoubtedly Cézanne also preferred the pencil because it was so accessible.

He enriched most of his pencil drawings with color. He did not use it to fill in the outlines of objects but to indicate shadings and intensities. Eventually these drawings, with their hints of color, led to the watercolors.

I t was not until the late 1890s that Cézanne developed his own distinct watercolor style. It consisted of a careful pencil drawing on which he casually composed a harmony of color. The pencil lines placed and positioned the pictured objects, but the spots of color carried the true artistic message. Suspended above and covering the borders made by the pencil, they formed complexes of color in connection with the areas of the pages left white. Cézanne deliberately omitted from his watercolors what had formerly been essential to him: the various tones of light and dark.

By the late 1890s, figures and objects in Cézanne's watercolors were only intimated, their shapes bordered lightly with pencil. Fruit, trees, and other objects were given three dimensions through freely suspended spots of color. Only the main points of a painting's composition were sketched, just as an orchestral work arranged for piano only presents the main musical thought. Cézanne wanted to capture the composition's overall design, not its details.

In his watercolors, Cézanne never let small color areas mix, although they often touch. When they do, the colors remain transparent; the white of the paper shows through even the deepest shades. The character of each work thus consists of the tones applied side-by-side, not in the transition from one color to another or the intensity of any one color.

After 1895, the watercolor replaced the plain pencil drawing as the vehicle Cézanne chose to express his personality. It carried with it all the characteristics of his pictorial handwriting. The progress the artist made in his oil paintings can be traced in these watercolors: they have a similar construction, light is represented by the white of the paper, and blue—Cézanne's favorite and dominant color—unites figures and objects with space.

Cézanne's use of the color blue deserves a close study, for it played a major role in his art. This is especially apparent in his masterpiece, *The Great Bathers*. Here, blue predominates. The nude figures are pink and light blue. Even the trees are blue; sky and clouds can be distinguished from their leaves only by stages of very light yellow or pink. The scholar Charles Tolnay wrote that "this blue is not air, but more than that—a fluid material, thick and liquid at the same time, an element in which all substances adapt to one another."

Cézanne treated his watercolors with as little respect as his drawings. Their value was first recognized by his friends Renoir and Degas, and by collectors such as Victor Chocquet, Auguste Pellerin, and Count Isaac de Camondo. By 1905, Cézanne's watercolors had become famous. Vollard intended to organize a special exhibition of them, but because of the artist's death in 1906 he never did; it was not until 1963 that such an exhibition took place at the Knoedler Gallery in New York.

E arly in his career, Cézanne drew many figures and portraits; most frequently, however, he drew himself. His self-portraits were not psychological sketches. He was never concerned with exploring his hidden thoughts; not even his eyes reveal anything of his inner life. Narcissism was far from his mind. He drew himself simply because he was his own most patient model. And he drew himself as objectively as he would have sketched an apple or a bouquet of artificial flowers.

His son, Paul, born in 1872, was also a model for many of his drawings, each of which reveals Cézanne's great love for the boy. Yet Cézanne was as strict with his son as he was with his other models. He required absolute motionlessness. "Does an apple move?" he would demand when a model complained or fidgeted.

The faces in his drawings are those of lonely people whose lifeless rigidness and reservation seem to correspond with the same or similar characteristics in the artist himself. Cézanne gave the people he drew his own personality. Thus they cannot be considered representative of the individuals who sat for them. As Fritz Novotny has noted, "In presenting the human face, Cézanne has eliminated all psychological and emotional content in favor of the domineering artistic goal."

Nevertheless, the portraits are not completely devoid of human content. Although he was primarily interested in the architecture and construction of the human face, Cézanne often depicted an inner being as well. In the face of the disfigured Achille Emperaire is a quiet nobility that evokes respect as well as compassion.

Almost half of Cézanne's oeuvre is devoted to nature. He often spoke of nature as his only model. It was the starting point, means, and goal of his artistic expression. "I paint what I see," he stated simply. But he was interested in capturing more than just a view. He wanted to capture his "small experiences."

Many of his drawings are hasty sketches brought back from a walk. Others are carefully painted watercolors. Whether they are studies of a small forest or studies of a beach, they are always without figures—like still lifes. His tree studies, especially, are arabesques of geometric shapes, expressing more by what is missing than by what is apparent.

VIEW OF THE JAS DE BOUFFAN

Cézanne sketched most of his landscapes in the same few places. He made famous the Jas de Bouffan, Mont Sainte-Victoire, the village of L'Estaque near Marseilles, and the gothic Château Noire and the Bibémus quarry outside of Aix. Located on a bay surrounded by sharp reefs, L'Estaque became an exceptional and inexhaustible source for his sketches. "It looks like playing cards," Cézanne wrote about the village to Pissarro in 1876. "Red roofs in front of the blue ocean."

Cézanne did not try to reconstruct nature in his works. Instead, he attempted to determine nature's constructive elements. "Whether I drew sketches or painted," he once said, "they were all constructions after nature which were based on meanings, feelings, and perfection of the model." Nature only provided the inspiration.

Cézanne's unique concept of line can best be seen in his landscapes. The areas he left blank in these drawings and watercolors do not reflect his inabilities; rather, they embody the logical, well-thought-out consequence of his ideas about arrangement. Moreover, they give the observer a chance to use his or her imagination. This is the same approach poet Paul Valéry had in mind when he said, "I write only one half of the poem; the other half is written by the reader."

The eternal values of nature, not its transitional ones, were the focus of Cézanne's attention. The objects he sketched and painted express tranquility and silence. Those that were uncertain, temporary, or unbalanced had no value to him.

He looked for the typical, not the specific. When painting Mont Sainte-Victoire, for example, he did not see the mountain landmark of his homeland but a symbol of stability, consistency, and eternity. In Cézanne's paintings, the ocean is always immobile, the houses separate and calm, the trees gathered together in a close mass.

The same sense of tranquility may be found in Cézanne's still lifes. In many ways, he preferred painting still lifes to painting almost anything else. They were not as subject to as many quick changes as objects found in a landscape; illuminated by a neutral light filtering through a studio window, a still life seemed more balanced, easier to understand. Still lifes dominated Cézanne's work toward the end of his career. Fruit, vases, and tablecloths were favorite subjects. The artist seldom included flowers because they wilted so quickly. They show up more frequently in his watercolors, which required a faster working pace.

Cézanne did not forsake the human figure in his later years. One of his most famous paintings is *The Card Players* (1890-1892), which was preceded by five studies and a large number of sketches. The profiled figure in the right of the painting was prepared with particular earnestness in a carefully worked-out drawing.

Cézanne did not have to go far for models for this painting or any other. Many came from among the workers on his family's estate or from nearby villages. A favorite was his gardener, Paulet Vallier, whom Cézanne described as patient and quiet "as an apple."

As a mature artist, Cézanne returned to a theme he had pursued in his youth: the nude in landscape. In the 1870s he had begun a series of paintings of nude bathers. Now uncomfortable in the presence of unclothed models, Cézanne relied on sketches he had drawn years before at the Atelier Suisse. He told his friends that he was using these sketches because he was too old to "undress a woman in order to paint her." More likely, he was unable to overcome his feelings of sexual inadequacy and shame.

When the sketches proved insufficient for his needs, Cézanne asked a young photographer to supply him with nude portraits. Even these were not enough, and he finally recognized that it was essential to work once again with live models. He decided to find one. "What, Mr. Cézanne, a naked woman?" his friend Vollard gasped when he heard of the artist's plans. Cézanne assured him that the model would be an "old maid." Soon even she was dismissed.

Cézanne returned to studying his old nude drawings, most notably those he had drawn of sculptures at the Louvre. He drew them again, sometimes lightly, sometimes with great precision and purpose, as he tried to solve new compositional problems. In these copies his line is freer, probably because he was not distracted by the need to look directly at the statues.

The nudes that appear in the finished paintings of the bathers series serve only as compositional elements. They express nothing of Cézanne himself, nothing of his unsatisfied longing or hidden sensuality. The artist used the figures to explore the harmony between humankind and nature, between the material and the immaterial worlds. He was not interested either in delving into or expressing his own inner world. He was attempting a balance, an integration of style and subject—and he succeeded magnificently.

The spiritual message of Cézanne's drawings has evoked a different echo from each succeeding generation of artists. His work has been interpreted and reinterpreted, for it fits into no single category. Yet it continues to challenge new artists with its freshness.

"I am too old and I came too soon," Cézanne once said. "But I mark the way and others will follow."

SELECTED BIBLIOGRAPHY

Badt, K. *Die Kunst Cézannes*. Munich, 1956.

Berthold, G. *Cézanne und die alten Meister.* Stuttgart, 1958.

Cháppuis, A. *Dessins*. Lausanne, 1957.

--------- *Die Zeichnungen von Paul Cézanne in Kupferstichkabinett Basel* (two volumes). Olten and Lausanne, 1962.

Dunstan, B. *Painting Methods of the Impressionists*. New York, 1976.

Elgar, F. *Cézanne*. New York and Washington, 1975.

Guerry, L. *Cézanne et l'expression de l'espace*. Paris, 1950.

Lindsay, J. *Cézanne: his life and art*. London, 1969.

Mandl, J. and Novotny, F. *Ausstellungskatalog*. Vienna, 1961.

Murphy, R., and the editors of Time-Life Books, *The World of Cézanne 1839-1906*. New York, 1968.

Novotny, F. *Cézanne*. London, 1961.

--------- *Cézanne als Zeichner*. Vienna, 1950.

--------- *Cézanne und das Ende der wissenschaftlichen Perspektive*. Vienna, 1938.

Perruchot, H. *Briefe*. Zurich, 1962.

---------- *Cézanne*. Paris, 1958.

Rewald, J. *Carnet des dessins*. Paris, 1951.

Schmidt, G. *Aquarelles de P. Cézanne*. Basel, 1952.

Shapiro, M. and Reff, Th. *Cézanne Watercolours* (an exhibition catalogue). New York, 1963.

Taillandier, Y. *P. Cézanne*. New York.

Venturi, L. *Cézanne, son art—son oeuvre*. Paris, 1935.

CATALOGUE

—Cover—

BATHING PEOPLE UNDER FOOTBRIDGE (See Plate IV)

—Frontispiece—

THE GARDENER VALLIER (See Plate XIV)

Black-and-White Plates

—1—

HEAD OF THE PAINTER ACHILLE EMPERAIRE, c. 1867-1870
Coal, 43.2 x 31.8 cm.
Kupferstichkabinett der Oeffentlichen Kunstsammlung
(Copper Engravings Cabinet)
Kunstmuseum, Basel

—2—

PAIR IN THE GARDEN, c. 1870
Pencil, 15.3 x 10.4 cm.
Albertina, Vienna

—3—

READING MAN, c. 1865
Pencil, 12 x 9 cm.
Private collection, Basel

—4—

GROUP OF FAUNS AND SATYRS ATTACKING A NUDE WOMAN,
c. 1875-1885
Pencil, 12.7 x 22.2 cm.
The Art Institute, Chicago

—5—

COMPOSITION WITH FIVE FIGURES, c. 1875-1885
Pencil, 13.5 x 21.5 cm.
The Art Institute, Chicago

—6—

CAMILLE PISSARRO GOES PAINTING, c. 1874-1877
Pencil, 22 x 13.2 cm.
The Louvre, Paris

—7—

STUDY WITH SELF-PORTRAIT, c. 1875-1895
Pencil, 49.5 x 32.2 cm.
Museum Boymans-van-Beuningen, Rotterdam

—8—

FOUR BATHING WOMEN, c. 1879-1882
Pencil and black chalk, 20.3 x 22.3 cm.
Museum Boymans-van-Beuningen, Rotterdam

—9—

BATHING WOMAN, c. 1878-1882
Pencil, 20.6 x 13 cm.
Museum Boymans-van-Beuningen, Rotterdam

—10—

PORTRAIT OF THE ARTIST'S SON, c. 1880
Pencil, 27.3 x 23 cm.
Albertina, Vienna

—11—

STUDY AFTER AN ANTIQUE (APOLLON LYCIEN), c. 1882
Pencil, 20.9 x 12.1 cm.
Kupferstichkabinett der Oeffentlichen Kunstsammlung
(Copper Engravings Cabinet)
Kunstmuseum, Basel

—12—

PORTRAIT OF HORTENSE CÉZANNE, c. 1883-1886
Pencil, 48.5 x 32.2 cm.
Museum Boymans-van-Beuningen, Rotterdam

—13—

STILL LIFE WITH CARAFE, c. 1888-1892
Pencil, 19.9 x 12 cm.
Kupferstichkabinett der Oeffentlichen Kunstsammlung
(Copper Engravings Cabinet)
Kunstmuseum, Basel

—14—

LANDSCAPE IN THE PROVENCE, c. 1887-1888
Pencil, 12.5 x 20.3 cm.
Kupferstichkabinett der Oeffentlichen Kunstsammlung
(Copper Engravings Cabinet)
Kunstmuseum, Basel

—15—

PORTRAIT OF HORTENSE CÉZANNE, c. 1875-1885
Pencil, 12.6 x 21.7 cm.
Collection of Leigh B. Block, Chicago

—16—

HERCULES, STUDY AFTER PUGET, c. 1888-1895
Pencil, 30 x 47 cm.
Museum Boymans-van-Beuningen, Rotterdam

—17—

CUPID, STUDY AFTER PUGET, c. 1888-1895
Pencil, 31 x 48.2 cm.
Museum Boymans-van-Beuningen, Rotterdam

—18—

ROWER, c. 1865-1870
Pencil, 22.7 x 29.9 cm.
Museum Boymans-van-Beuningen, Rotterdam

—19—

HEAD OF A BOY, c. 1896
Pencil, 37.6 x 30.2 cm.
Museum Boymans-van-Beuningen, Rotterdam

—20—

PORTRAIT OF HORTENSE CÉZANNE, c. 1895-1896
Pencil, 17.2 x 12 cm.
Collection of H. Berggruen, Paris

—21—

THE SMOKER, c. 1890-1899
Pencil, 26.5 x 26 cm.
Museum Boymans-van-Beuningen, Rotterdam

—22—

STUDY, c. 1875-1885
Pencil, 22.2 x 28.5 cm.
Museum of Fine Arts, Budapest

—23—

PILLOW, c. 1887
Pencil, 30 x 22.5 cm.
Collection of H. Berggruen, Paris

—24—

OPEN BED, c. 1870-1880
Pencil, 27 x 19 cm.
Collection of H. Berggruen, Paris

—25—

SELF-PORTRAIT, c. 1878-1880
Pencil, 30 x 25 cm.
Museum of Fine Arts, Budapest

—26—

CHESTNUT LANE AT THE JAS DE BOUFFAN, c. 1884-1887
Pencil, 30.7 x 47.8 cm.
Museum Boymans-van-Beuningen, Rotterdam

—27—

SKETCH OF A LANDSCAPE, c. 1895-1900
Pencil, 47.6 x 31.8 cm.
National Gallery, Prague

—28—

SKETCH OF A LANDSCAPE, c. 1895-1900
Pencil, 52 x 32.3 cm.
National Gallery, Prague

—29—

CLUSTER OF TREES AT THE BACK OF A LOW-LYING WALL,
c. 1895-1900
Pencil, 54.2 x 41.6 cm.
National Gallery, Prague

—30—

SKETCH OF A TREE, c. 1896-1900
Pencil, 31.3 x 47.5 cm.
National Gallery, Prague

—31—

VIEW OF TREES AND THE ROOF OF A HOUSE, c. 1883-1885
Pencil, 32.6 x 34.5 cm.
Museum Boymans-van-Beuningen, Rotterdam

—32—

PORTRAIT OF AMBROISE VOLLARD, c. 1898-1899
Pencil, 45.8 x 39.7 cm.
The Fogg Museum, Cambridge, Massachusetts

—33—

STUDY OF A TOMBSTONE, c. 1870
Watercolor drawing, 21.7 x 12.6 cm.
Museum Boymans-van-Beuningen, Rotterdam

—34—

THE APOTHEOSIS OF DELACROIX, c. 1875-1880
Watercolor drawing, 19.6 x 23 cm.
Collection of Dr. Fr. and Peter Nathan, Zurich

—35—

STILL LIFE, c. 1885-1888
Watercolor drawing, 23.8 x 31.8 cm.
Museum of Fine Arts, Budapest

—36—

BATHING MAN, c. 1879-1882
Watercolor drawing, 21.5 x 15.3 cm.
The Wadsworth Atheneum, Hartford, Connecticut

—37—

NUDE STUDY, c. 1885-1895
Pencil and wash, 63.5 x 49.4 cm.
The Fogg Museum, Cambridge, Massachusetts

—38—

CARD PLAYER, c. 1890-1892
Watercolor drawing, 48.5 x 36.3 cm.
Art Museum, Providence, Rhode Island

—39—

ROOFS IN L'ESTAQUE, c. 1883-1885
Watercolor, 31 x 47.5 cm.
Museum Boymans-van-Beuningen, Rotterdam

—40—

CASTLE OF MONTGEROULT, 1899
Watercolor, 44 x 55 cm.
Collection of H. Berggruen, Paris

—41—

FOREST HUT, c. 1888-1894
Watercolor, 44 x 29 cm.
Collection of H. Berggruen, Paris

—42—

LANDSCAPE, c. 1890-1894
Watercolor, 31.3 x 47.8 cm.
Museum of Fine Arts, Budapest

—43—

LANDSCAPE NEAR GALET, c. 1879-1882
Watercolor, 31.6 x 49 cm.
Collection of Mr. and Mrs. Alex M. Lewyt, New York

—44—

CUPID, c. 1888-1895
Watercolor drawing, 48 x 31.5 cm.
Museum of Finé Arts, Budapest

—45—

LANDSCAPE WITH ROOFS OF HOUSES, c. 1890-1900
Watercolor, 32.5 x 40 cm.
Museum Boymans-van-Beuningen, Rotterdam

—46—

TREES AND BUILDINGS, c. 1900
Watercolor, 22.5 x 48 cm.
Museum Boymans-van-Beuningen, Rotterdam

—47—

MONT SAINTE-VICTOIRE, c. 1890
Watercolor and charcoal, 31.5 x 47.5 cm.
Courtauld Institute of Art, London

—48—

VIEW OF MONT SAINT-VICTOIRE, c. 1895-1900
Watercolor, 38.7 x 49.4 cm.
The Fogg Museum, Cambridge, Massachusetts

—49—

PATH BETWEEN TREES, c. 1890-1896
Watercolor and chalk, 43 x 31 cm.
Collection of J. Spreiregen, Paris

—50—

COAT OVER A CHAIR, c. 1890-1895
Watercolor drawing, 45.7 x 26 cm.
Collection of Dr. W. Feilchenfeldt, Zurich

—51—

SELF-PORTRAIT, c. 1894
Watercolor, 26.3 x 21.9 cm.
Collection of Dr. W. Feilchenfeldt, Zurich

—52—

LANDSCAPE, c. 1890-1892
Watercolor, 31 x 27 cm.
Museum Boymans-van-Beuningen, Rotterdam

—53—

SKULL, c. 1885-1890
Watercolor, 31 x 47 cm.
Collection of Dr. W. Feilchenfeldt, Zurich

—54—

THREE SKULLS, c . 1900-1904
Watercolor, 45.9 x 62.9 cm.
The Art Institute, Chicago

—55—

BATHING WOMEN, c. 1900-1906
Watercolor, 21 x 27 cm.
Private collection, Zurich

—56—

STUDY OF A TREE, c. 1885-1890
Watercolor, 27 x 45 cm.
House of Arts, Zurich

—57—

HUT, c. 1880
Watercolor and black chalk, 31 x 47.5 cm.
Coutauld Institute of Art, London

—58—

VIEW FROM THE JAS DE BOUFFAN TOWARD MONT SAINTE-VICTOIRE,
1886
Watercolor, 46.5 x 30.5 cm.
Collection of H . Berggruen, Paris

—59—

L'ESTAQUE, c. 1895-1900
Watercolor and pencil, 49 x 30 cm.
Art Museum, Providence, Rhode Island ·

—60—

CHATEAU NOIR, c. 1895-1900
Watercolor and pencil, 36 x 52.6 cm.
Museum Boymans-van-Beuningen, Rotterdam

—61—

CHESTNUT TREES, c. 1900
Watercolor drawing, 32.6 x 49.6 cm.
Art Museum, Providence, Rhode Island

—62—

AT THE EDGE OF THE FOREST, c. 1900-1904
Watercolor, 32 x 49.5 cm.
Collection of H. Berggruen, Paris

—63—

BRIDGE, 1906
Watercolor, 40.6 x 53.3 cm.
Cincinnati Art Museum, Cincinnati, Ohio

—64—

TREES, c. 1900
Watercolor drawing, 47 x 30.5 cm.
Collection of Dr. W. Feilchenfeldt, Zurich

—65—

TREES, c. 1890-1900
Watercolor drawing, 32 x 49 cm.
Collection of Dr. W. Feilchenfeldt, Zurich

—66—

STILL LIFE WITH PEARS, c. 1890-1894
Watercolor, 12.6 x 20.8 cm.
Museum Boymans-van-Beuningen, Rotterdam

Color Plates

—I—

LOVE FIGHT, c. 1875-1876
Watercolor, 15 x 22 cm.
Collection of Dr. W. Feilchenfeldt, Zurich

—II—

TREE AT THE JAS DE BOUFFAN, c. 1880
Watercolor, 31.5 x 49 cm.
Collection of H. Berggruen, Paris

—III—

MONT MARSEILLEVEYRE, c. 1882-1885
Watercolor, 29 x 45.5 cm.
House of Arts, Zurich

—IV—

BATHING PEOPLE UNDER FOOTBRIDGE, 1895
Watercolor, 21 x 27 cm.
Museum of Modern Art, New York

—V—

GREEN PITCHER, c. 1885-1900
Watercolor, 19.5 x 23.2 cm.
The Louvre, Paris

—VI—

CARD PLAYER, c. 1895-1900
Watercolor, 48.5 x 36.3 cm.
Collection of Robert von Hirsch, Basel

—VII—

STREET LINED WITH CHESTNUT TREES, c. 1885-1900
Watercolor, 47.8 x 31.7 cm.
Private collection, Switzerland

—VIII—

STREET IN CHANTILLY, c. 1888
Watercolor, 20 x 12 cm.
Collection of David M. Levy, New York

—IX—

MILL AT THE RIVER, c. 1900-1906
Watercolor, 32 x 49.5 cm.
Hall of Arts, Hamburg

—X—

HOUSE IN THE PROVENCE, c. 1890
Watercolor, 42.5 x 57 cm.
Collection of F. H. Hirschland, New York

—XI—

FLOWERS IN GREEN VASE, c. 1885-1895
Watercolor, 48 x 31.3 cm.
Collection of Paul M. Hirschland, New York

—XII—

STILL LIFE WITH GREEN MELON, c. 1900
Watercolor, 32 x 48 cm.
Collection of Robert von Hirsch, Basel

—XIII—

STILL LIFE WITH APPLES, c. 1890-1900
Watercolor, 47.7 x 63 cm.
Museum of Art History, Vienna

—XIV—

THE GARDENER VALLIER, c. 1902-1906
Watercolor, 48 x 31 cm.
Collection of H. Berggruen, Paris

—XV—

STILL LIFE, c. 1904-1906
Watercolor, 45 x 59.7 cm.
Coutauld Institute of Art, London

—XVI—

SELF-PORTRAIT, c. 1894
Watercolor, 26.3 x 21.9 cm.
Collection of Dr. W. Feilchenfeldt, Zurich

THE PLATES

12

13

16

IV.

19

20

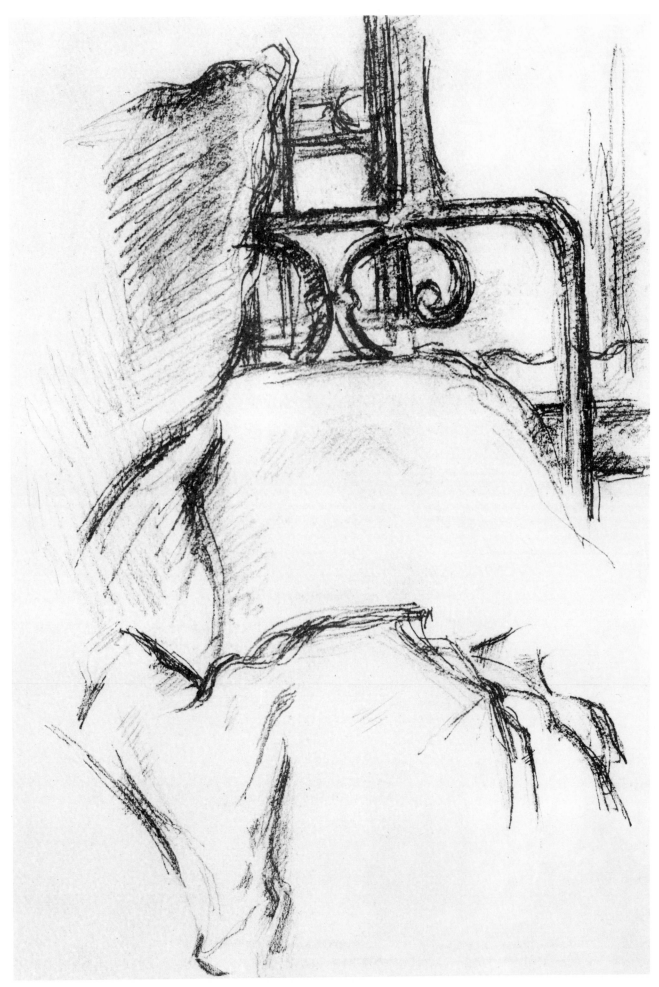

VI.

28

VII.

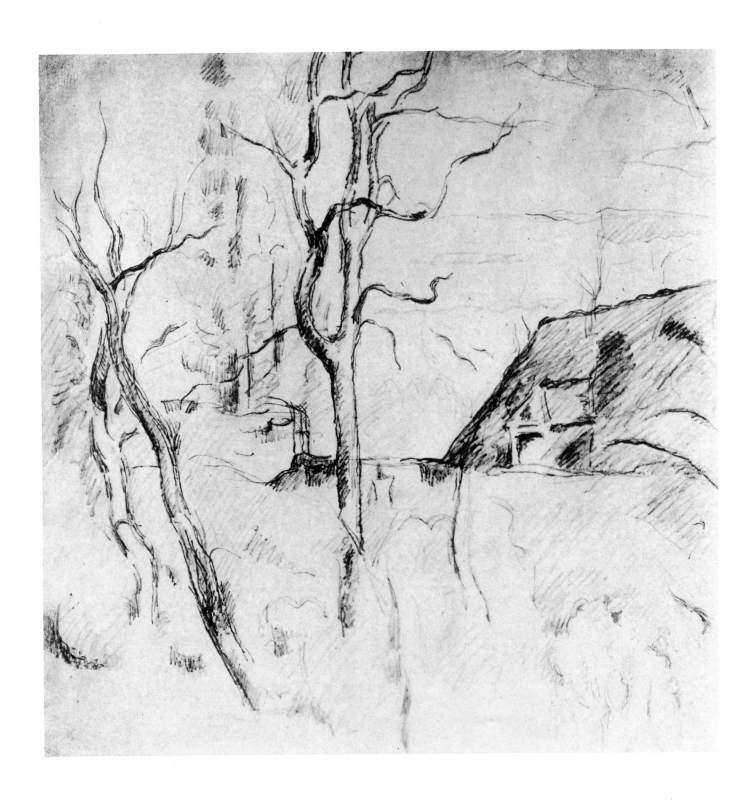

VIII.

45

46

XVI.